Fairfield P.N.E.U. School
(Backwell) Ltd.,
Farleigh Road,
Backwell, Bristol.

WEATHER PROJECTS

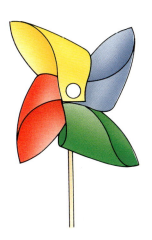

Fairfield P.N.E.U. School
(Backwell) Ltd.,
Farleigh Road,
Backwell, Bristol.

WEATHER PROJECTS

Sharon McCormick

CHERRYTREE BOOKS

551.6
May'94

A Cherrytree Book

Designed and produced by
Pemberton Press Ltd

First published 1992
by Cherrytree Press Ltd
a subsidiary of
The Chivers Company Ltd
Windsor Bridge Road
Bath, Avon BA2 3AX

Copyright © Cherrytree Press Ltd 1992

British Library Cataloguing in Publication Data

McCormick, Sharon
　Weather Projects
　1. Meteorology
　I. Title II. Series
　551.5

ISBN 0-7451-5120-5

All rights reserved. No part of this publication may be reproduced, stored in a retrieval system, or transmitted. in any form or by any means without the prior permission in writing of the publisher, nor be otherwise circulated in any form of binding or cover other than that in which it is published and without a similar condition including this condition being imposed on the subsequent purchaser.

Contents

What is Weather?

Sunlight	8
Shadow Clocks and Sundials	10
The Seasons	12
Air Pressure	13
Hot or Cold Air?	16
Evaporation and Condensation	18
Clouds	20
Rain, Snow and Sleet	21
Hail, Fog and Smog	22
The Water Cycle	23
What is Wind?	24

Measuring Weather

Measuring Wind	28
Rain Gauge	30
Make a Rainbow	31
Thunder and Lightning	32
Measuring Pressure	34
Measuring Temperature	36
Nature's Forecasters	37
Weather Chart	38
Harnessing the Weather	40
Safety Notes	42
Words to Remember	44
Books to Read	46
Index	47

Getting Started

Before you do any experiments, take a few minutes to read the Safety Notes on page 42 at the back of the book. None of these experiments is dangerous, but you will need to be careful in handling some of the household items. If you read something that is not clear to you, or if you have any questions about an experiment, ask an adult or an older friend for some help.

Some of the experiments have a marker that looks like this:

This means that you should ask permission to do the experiment. You may need help from an adult.

DO NOT do experiments marked

unless an adult is available to help you.

In all of the experiments, try to follow the directions as closely as possible. For the experiments in which you need to make something, the drawings will help you understand more about the things you are building. Most of the experiments will work better if you follow the drawings as closely as you can. If an experiment doesn't work first time, try to work out why and then try again.

What is Weather?

Is the sun shining today? Is it warm or cool outside? Did it rain yesterday? All these things are part of what we call the weather.

Weather is the state of the atmosphere at a given time and place. That means how hot or cold it is, how wet or dry, clear or cloudy. The average yearly weather of a particular place is called its climate.

The five main building blocks of the weather are temperature, air pressure, moisture, clouds and wind. Each one is constantly changing. All five are continuously interacting with each other.

Sunlight

The sun, our closest star, is about 150,000,000 kilometres (93,000,000 miles) away. Without its heat and light, all life on Earth would die.

Green plants need sunlight to grow and make their food. The plants are the beginning of the food chain. They are eaten by animals. All living things, including human beings, feed on plants, or on animals that have eaten plants.

You can prove that green plants need sunlight to live.

You will need
a piece of card about 30 cm (12 in) square
a patch of grass

No sun, no life
1. Place a piece of card over a patch of grass.
2. Leave it for a few days, then check the grass underneath. You will see that the grass has started to turn yellow because it could not get any sunlight. The grass will slowly return to normal if you leave the card off.

Because sunlight is so important, plants actually grow towards the light.

1. Plant some grass seeds in a little potting compost on two saucers or other shallow containers.

2. Cut a hole in the side of a box.

3. After the seeds sprout, place the box over one saucer. Leave the other saucer in full light. Remember to dampen the soil if it becomes dry.

4. After a week, check the plants. Did the sprouts covered by the box grow differently? In what way?

You will need
grass seed
potting compost
2 saucers
a box big enough to fit over one saucer
scissors

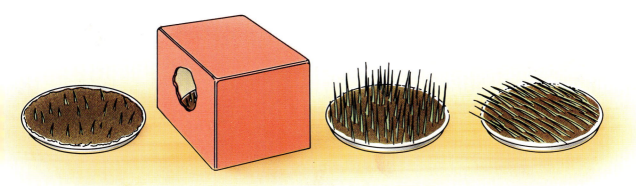

During the day the sun heats the land, oceans and lakes. In the evening the land lets go of its warmth quickly, but the water stores heat, losing its warmth much more slowly. You can see and feel this for yourself.

1. Fill one container with dry soil and the other with water.

2. Put them in the refrigerator until both are about the same temperature. Then set them in a sunny spot, indoors or out.

3. In about two hours, touch each of the containers. Is the soil warmer than the water?

4. Now, move them to a spot out of the sun. Which one cools down more quickly?

You will need
2 clean metal containers
soil
water

Shadow Clocks and Sundials

As the Earth turns on its axis during the day, the sun appears to move across the sky. The position of the sun helps us tell what time of day it is. Before clocks were invented, our ancestors told the time with sundials, which use shadows.

You can make a simple sundial.

1. On a sunny day, hammer a nail into the wood.
2. On the first day, use a clock or watch to mark where the shadow falls at each hour or half-hour.
3. The next day, you can tell the time without using a clock. Just check the shadows on your sundial.

You will need
a piece of wood
 15 cm (6 in) square and
 1 cm (⅜ in) thick
a long nail
a hammer
a clock or watch

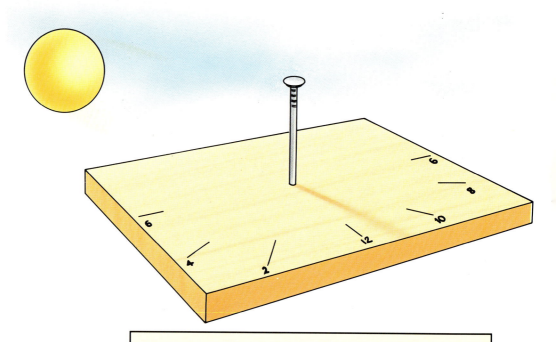

Shadows
Have you ever looked at your own shadow as you walked along the pavement? Is it longer at 9 o'clock in the morning than it is at mid-day? Do you know why?

At mid-day the sun is at its highest. It casts a much shorter shadow than early in the morning or late in the afternoon. Then its rays slant more.

1. Shine a torch directly down on to a salt shaker (or any oblong object). You will see there is hardly any shadow at all.

You will need
a salt shaker
a torch

2. Now, move the torch slowly down. Keep the light directly on the object. You will see the shadow grow longer as you move the torch.

The Seasons

The time of day is not the only thing affected by the sun. It also controls the seasons of the year.

While the Earth spins on its axis, making one spin each day, it also circles the sun. Each trip round the sun takes one year.

When the top half of the Earth, called the northern hemisphere, is tilted towards the sun, it has summer. When it leans away from the sun, it has winter. People in the southern hemisphere have opposite seasons. For example, when it is spring in Europe, it is autumn in Australia.

Seasons in shadows
Shadows can show us the difference between the sun's position in winter and in summer.

1. One winter's day, place a long stick in the ground. Mark its shadow every hour on a piece of paper.

2. Later, on a sunny summer's day, place the stick in the same place and mark the shadows again. What differences do you see between the two?

You will need
a long stick such as a cricket stump
paper and pencil

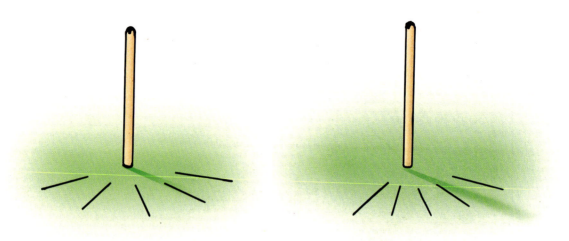

Air Pressure

The air between Earth and space is called the atmosphere. It is a mixture of gases made up of countless particles called molecules. The air is held near the Earth by gravity.

Although we cannot feel it, air has weight, or pressure. The air presses on everything around us, and on us. We do not feel its weight because we have the same pressure inside our bodies as outside.

Even though we can't feel it, we can see air pressure in action. Hot air is lighter than cold air. Its pressure is lower.

1. Pour 5–10 cm (2–4 in) of very hot, but not boiling, water into a clean, plastic drinks bottle.

2. Let some of the steam escape. Then screw the top on very quickly. Did the bottle cave in? Do you know why?

You will need
a small plastic drinks bottle with a screw-on top
very hot tap water

The heat of the water made the air expand and forced some of it out of the bottle. Because so many air molecules escaped in the steam, the air that was left inside the bottle was thinner than the regular air pressure outside the bottle. When you put the cap on, no more air could get in. The bottle was squashed by the pressure from the outside.

This air pressure experiment should be done outdoors or over the kitchen sink.

You will need
a cork
a plastic drinks bottle
a skewer
a straw
water

1. Make a hole in a cork. Fit a drinking straw into the hole.

2. Half fill a bottle with water. Push the cork into the top so that it fits tightly. Make sure the straw reaches well down into the water in the bottle.

3. Blow through the straw as hard as you can. Then take your face away very quickly.

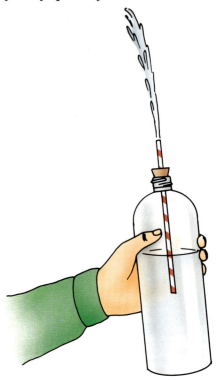

By blowing into the straw, you have pushed more air into the bottle. When you stop blowing, the pressure forces the extra air out of the bottle the only way it can go -- back up the straw. It takes some of the water with it. So it is like your own personal fountain.

You can stop water from flowing using air pressure too.

1. Position a funnel in the neck of the jar. Seal it tightly with plasticine.

2. Fill the funnel with water. What happens? Why do you think the water won't run through?

3. Now make a hole in the plasticine. What happens now?

You will need
a glass jar with a narrow neck
a funnel
a lump of plasticine
a skewer
water

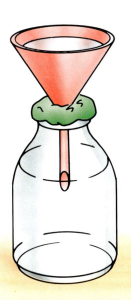

The water flows into the jar because the pressure is now the same inside and outside the jar. That is why you need to make two holes before you can pour liquid from a tin.

Hot or Cold Air?

Did you know that warm air rises? Heat makes the air molecules move faster, and the faster they go, the farther apart they spread. When the same molecules cool down, they slow down and come closer together again. Because cold air has more molecules, it weighs more than the same amount of warm air. It is heavier, so it shrinks and sinks. This causes the warmer air below it to rise. These movements in the air help to cause changes in the weather.

You will need
heavy paper
a pencil
a length of cotton

We can watch warm air rising
1. Draw a spiral on the paper. Cut carefully along the line of the spiral.
2. Thread a piece of cotton through the "snake's head". Hang it above a radiator and watch what happens.

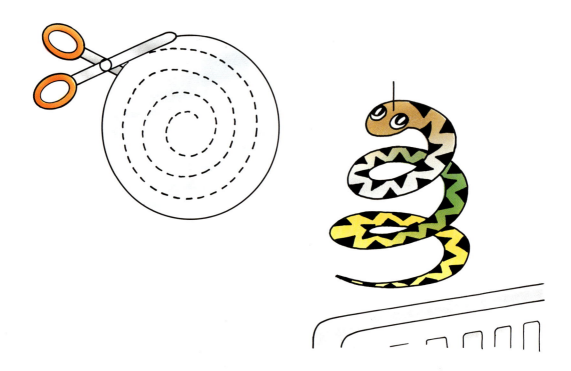

A "draught detector" shows the effects of cold air as well as warm air.

1. Push the pencil through the hole in an ordinary cotton reel.

2. Push the straight pin through a paper straw to attach it to the top of the pencil.

3. Glue or tape the small piece of paper folded in half to one end of the straw. Place a paper clip at the other end. The straw must balance exactly.

4. Place your draught detector over a radiator or a warm cooker. Then move it to a spot below an open window. What happens? Does the warm draught make the paper end go up or down? Does the cold draught do the same?

You will need
- a pencil with a rubber at one end
- a cotton reel
- a straight pin
- a straw (a paper one works best)
- a piece of paper 8x5 cm (3x2 in)
- sellotape or glue
- a paper clip

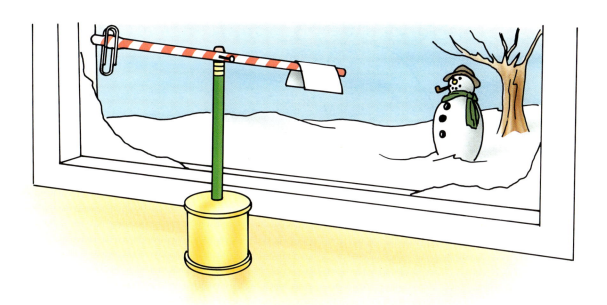

Because the warm air is lighter, it rises. It is trapped under the paper and pushes the straw up. The cold air is heavier. Its weight pushes on the paper and the straw moves down.

Evaporation and Condensation

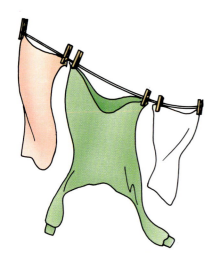

When a liquid changes to a gas, it evaporates. Every second, about 15 million tonnes of moisture evaporates from the Earth's surface in the heat of the sun. When the molecules in gas cool, they come back together and form a liquid (or a solid if it is very cold). This process is called condensation.

Warm air can hold more water vapour than cold air. When air holds all the water vapour it can, it is said to be saturated. The amount of moisture in the air is called the humidity. If you put wet clothes on the line, will they dry more quickly if the humidity is high or if it is low?

You can watch evaporation in action.

You will need
2 identical bowls
washable felt-tipped pen

1. Fill two bowls with the same amount of water in each. Mark the water level on both bowls.

2. Place one bowl in a sunny window and the other in a dark corner or cupboard.

3. Every day for one week, mark the new water level. Which bowl evaporated faster? Why?

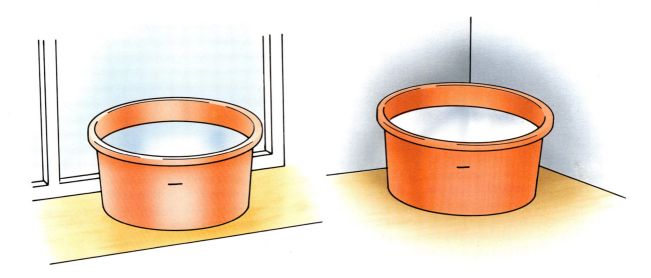

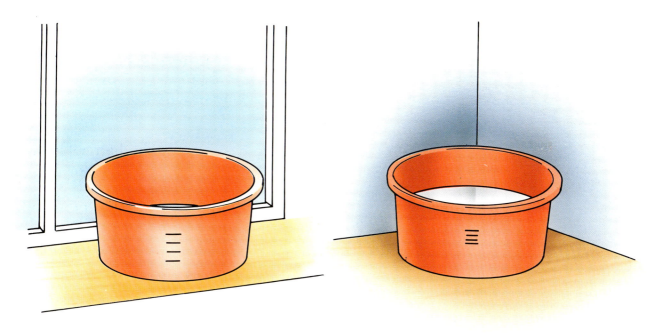

You can also watch condensation at work.

1. Fill a bowl with water from the hot tap. Hold a cold plate over the bowl. After a minute, turn the plate over. Is it covered with water droplets? Why does the water condense onto the plate?

2. Breathe hard onto a mirror or a cold window pane. What happens? Is the cloudy effect actually tiny drops of water?

3. Fill a metal mug with ice cubes. How long does it take for the outside of the tin to be covered with droplets?

All three of these experiments are about warmth meeting cold.

You will need
a bowl
a cold plate
hot tap water
a mirror
a metal camping mug
ice cubes

Clouds

Clouds form when warm, moisture-laden air rises as its molecules expand. The molecules then cool off again and crowd together. The colder the temperature, the less water vapour the air can hold. When the air becomes too cool to carry its load, the vapour begins to condense into water droplets. A cloud is created.

Clouds come in many forms. There are three basic types: cirrus, cumulus and stratus.

1. Cirrus clouds are white wisps, too high and too thin to cast a shadow.

2. Cumulus clouds are thick and puffy, and cast a dark shadow on the Earth below. Sometimes they become towering thunderclouds.

3. Stratus cloud spreads an even sheet across the sky. From the ground it looks grey. From an aeroplane, its top side looks like a sea of white cotton wool.

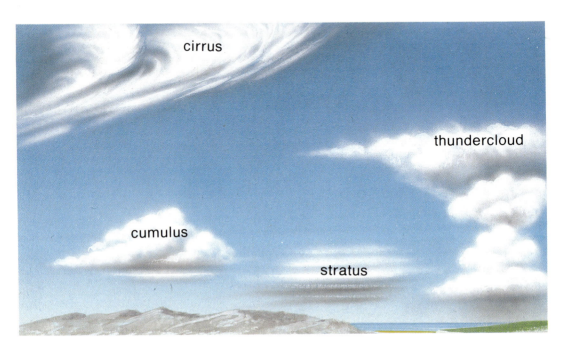

Rain, Snow and Sleet

When water on Earth evaporates, the water vapour mixes with other gases in the air and rises. The air cools as it rises and the water vapour condenses. Clouds form from the tiny droplets. As the clouds thicken, the droplets combine to make larger drops. When the drops become heavy enough, they fall from the clouds as rain.

If the temperature in the clouds is below freezing, the drops form tiny crystals of ice. When these crystals are heavy enough to fall, they leave the clouds as snowflakes. If the air between the clouds and the ground is cold, the flakes fall as snow. If the air temperature is warmer, the flakes melt as they fall, and hit the ground as raindrops. Sleet is a mixture of snow and rain.

Hail, Fog and Smog

Hail
Hailstones are hard balls of ice. They are made of numerous layers that form in thunderclouds. Ice crystals are tossed up and down in the turbulent clouds. More and more thicknesses of ice build up until the hailstones are heavy enough to fall.
Hail generally occurs in spring and summer. The hailstones are too big to melt, even in the warmer air between the clouds and the ground.

Fog and Smog
A cloud that forms close to the ground is called fog. It is made in the same way as clouds in the sky, by the condensation of water vapour.

When warm moist air collects around smoke particles in dirty city air, smog is formed. Its name comes from putting together the words "smoke" and "fog". It is very unhealthy. Since it is caused by pollution, we all need to learn what we can do to help clean up our air.

The Water Cycle

Water rises and falls in a never-ending journey called the water cycle. The amount of water is the same today as it was when the Earth was formed millions of years ago. It just goes round and round.

How does the water cycle work? The heat from the sun causes water to rise and evaporate from the oceans, rivers and lakes, and from the land. The warm air rises and cools.

As water vapour begins to cool, it forms clouds. Under the right conditions, the water returns to Earth as rain or snow. Then the water cycle begins again.

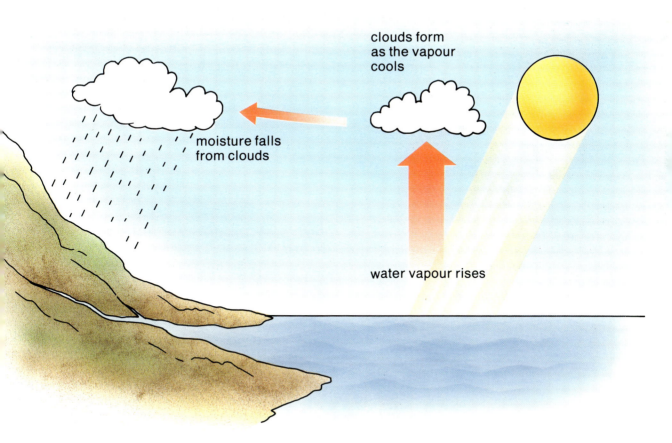

What is Wind?

Wind is moving air. The Earth's atmosphere is heated by the sun. The warm air rises, causing the atmospheric pressure to decrease. As the pressure falls, air rushes from a high-pressure area to the low-pressure area to try to even it out. The rushing air is wind. The greater the difference between the high- and low-pressure areas, the stronger the wind.

How many kinds of winds can you name? There are local winds, global winds, sea breezes and monsoons.

The two most destructive winds are tornadoes and hurricanes. An average tornado is usually less than one kilometre wide, but the whirling tube of wind is so strong, it destroys almost everything in its path. Most tornadoes occur when the air is hot and humid. A thick dark cloud forms and air inside the bottom edge begins to rotate. This spinning air forms thin, rapidly turning masses of cloud. A funnel drops down out of the clouds. If it touches Earth, it stirs up a huge cloud of dust. As it snakes its way along the ground, it can lift trees and caravans, and cause houses to explode.

Hurricanes are areas of low air pressure. They develop over the ocean in the tropics. Hot air laden with water vapour begins to rise. Then this rising air starts to spin in the Earth's rotation.

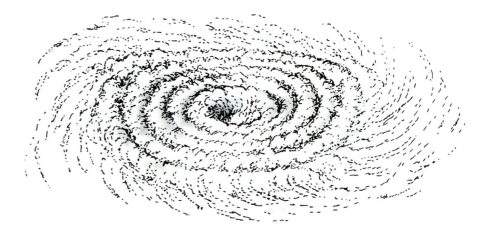

We can see the wind at work as it blows autumn leaves down the pavement or when it whips a flag out straight from its pole. But even on a windless day, you can study how moving air acts. This experiment uses a lighted candle, so be sure to ask permission. Make sure the candle is firmly anchored in a candlestick or stuck down with melted wax.

1. If you place a lighted candle 15 cm (6 in) in front of you and blow, it will go out, won't it? Of course.

2. But what happens if you place a tall bottle or glass between you and the candle and try again? The flame still goes out. The bottle splits the stream of air but it joins up again on the other side and blows out the candle. Land masses such as hills or mountains split the wind in a similar way.

You will need
1 short candle
matches
a tall bottle or glass

You will need
a piece of art paper 12cm (5 in) square
a piece of thin dowelling 20–30cm (8–12 in) long
a large drawing pin
scissors

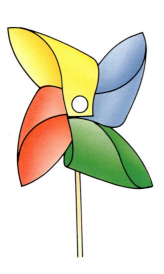

Make a windmill

1. Trace this square shape on to a piece of stiff paper. Copy the markings. Colour or paint your windmill if you like.

2. Cut out the square. Then cut along the four dotted lines and make tiny holes through the five dots.

3. Bend the four corners towards the centre until the four outer dots line up. Glue them together. Be sure not to crease the paper.

4. Push a drawing pin through the glued-together holes and the centre hole to hold them all together loosely. Do not push the pin in too tightly or the windmill will not spin. Ask an adult to help if necessary.

5. Test your windmill by blowing straight at it and then blow from each side. If you anchor it outside where you can see it from inside, you'll be able to tell how windy it is without going outside.

Measuring Weather

Weather forecasters are not magicians or prophets. They have many tools to help them in their work. Meteorologists, as weather scientists are called, measure temperature, air pressure, sunshine, rain, clouds and wind speed. You can make or collect instruments to help you forecast the weather for your area.

Measuring Wind

The speed and the direction of the wind affect the weather. You can make instruments for collecting information about the wind.

You will need
a paper cup
a pencil with a rubber on the end
thick card
plasticine or glue
thin card
scissors
a straight (dressmaker's) pin
a compass
a felt-tipped pen

1. Take a paper cup and make a hole in the middle of the bottom.

2. Push the pointed end of the pencil into the hole. Fix the paper cup to a piece of thick card with plasticine or glue.

3. Cut two strips of thin card. The first should be 20cm (8 in) long. Make a point at one end. Cut a slit in the middle of the other end 5cm (2 in) deep. Cut the other card strip 7·5 × 5cm (3 × 2 in) long. Slip it into the slit on the first piece as shown.

4. Push a straight pin through the middle of the card arrow and into the pencil rubber.

5. Mark north, south, east and west on the paper cup. Take your wind vane outside. Keep a chart on the direction of the wind for a day or a week.

Make an anemometer

An instrument for measuring the speed of the wind is called an anemometer.

1. Take three paper cups. Paint one of them a bright colour. Then make two holes in each, on opposite sides of the cup, about 4cm (1½ in) from the top. Push a pencil or a piece of thin dowelling through the holes in each cup and fix them securely with plasticine or glue.

2. Push the pencils into the sides of a large cork so they are equally spaced around the cork. Take a nail that is longer than the cork and push it through the centre of the cork.

3. Put two washers on the end of the nail and hammer the nail into the top of a pole, such as a broom handle. Do not hammer the nail in too tightly or the anemometer will not be able to spin around easily.

4. Stick the pole into the ground outside. Use the brightly coloured cup as a guide. Count the number of complete turns your anemometer makes in 10 seconds, 30 seconds, and so on.

You will need
3 paper cups
bright-coloured paint
3 pencils (or 3 pieces of dowelling, each 18cm (7 in) long)
plasticine or glue
a large cork
a long nail
2 washers
a hammer
a pole (old broom handle or thick dowelling)

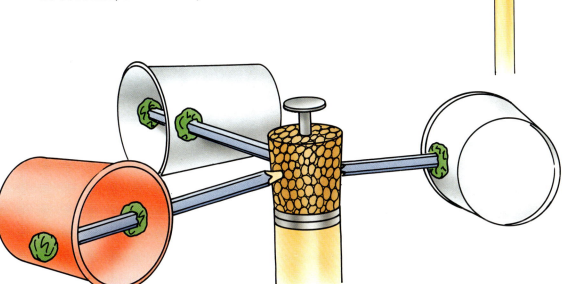

Rain Gauge

Do you get much rain where you live? Does it rain more during one season than another? You can measure the rainfall in your neighbourhood.

You will need
a large (2 litre) clean plastic bottle
a craft knife
a felt-tip pen
a ruler

1. Ask an adult to help you cut the top off a large plastic drinks bottle, about one quarter of the way down. Turn the top upside-down and fit it into the bottom part of the bottle. With a felt-tip pen, mark a scale on the bottle in centimetres or inches.

2. In a clear space outdoors (not under a bush or tree), dig a hole in the ground and put the bottle into it. Or secure the bottle above ground with heavy objects, such as bricks, so that the wind cannot blow it over.

3. Every day at the same time, or weekly on the same day, check the rainwater in the bottle. Keep a chart of the amount for a week or a month. Don't forget to pour the rainwater out of the bottle each time you check it.

Make a Rainbow

During or just after a rainstorm, you may see a rainbow in the sky. You can also see rainbows in bubbles of washing-up liquid, in light shining through cut glass, and in the spray from a garden hose or a waterfall.

You can make your own rainbow indoors.

1. Fill a flattish bowl with water. Place it in a sunny spot. Put a flat mirror in the water so that it rests against the side of the bowl. Position the bowl so that sunlight falls on it.

2. Hold a piece of white card in front of the mirror. Make sure the sunlight is reflected by the mirror on to the card. Move the card until you see rainbow colours. If you have trouble seeing the rainbow, adjust the angle of the mirror. Can you make the colours disappear? Place a magnifying glass between the mirror and the card. The glass bends the light. The colours merge and make white light again.

You will need
a flattish bowl such as a washing-up bowl
water
a flat unframed mirror
white card
a magnifying glass (optional)

Thunder and Lightning

There are 16 million thunderstorms around the world each year. They act as part of the Earth's air-conditioning system. They pump heat from the surface high into the atmosphere. There it is released into space. Without this action, temperatures on Earth might be much warmer than they are now, causing a very different world.

When a storm occurs, there is usually heavy rain, thunder and lightning. Lightning is a huge spark of electricity that travels between a cloud and the ground. Lightning is very dangerous so it is best to follow a few rules. Cars and metal buildings are good places to be during a thunderstorm. The metal conducts the electricity in the lightning to the ground. Keep away from wire fences and metal pipes. Water also conducts electricity. If you are in a swimming pool, get out at once. Lightning hits the highest object around, so don't stand under an isolated tree.

The heat from lightning makes the air around it expand suddenly. This expansion causes sound waves which reach our ears as thunder. When lightning is close, thunder sounds like a single, sharp crack. When the lightning is farther away, thunder is a rumbling noise, like a train coming.

If you don't mind a very small shock and a tingling in your hand, you can make your own mini-lightning.

You will need
leather-soled shoes
a carpet
a metal object

1. Put on a pair of leather-soled shoes and slide your feet across a wool or synthetic carpet.

2. Bring one finger close to a metal object, such as a doorknob. What happened? Did you see the tiny flash of light? Did you feel a small shock? Did you hear a mini-thunderclap? The shock is caused by static electricity built up through friction. Scientists think that lightning results from a build-up of friction between ice crystals and water droplets in the turbulent air currents in thunderclouds.

You can make a small spark of lightning in another way.

1. Take a fist-sized chunk of plasticine and press it into the middle of the metal tray so that it sticks firm.

2. Place the tray on the carpet. Holding the plasticine, rub the tray very hard in a circle a few times.

3. Holding the plasticine and not the tray, pick it up and hold the metal key close to one corner of the tray. Did you see a spark jump from the tray to the key? Did you hear the thunder? Try the experiment in a darkened room.

You will need
plasticine
a large metal tray
a carpet
a metal key

Measuring Pressure

Changes in the weather – from clear to cloudy, for instance – are caused by changes in air pressure.

A high pressure system is like a hill, with the greatest pressure in the centre. A low pressure system is like a valley between two mountains. The air in a low pressure system, also called a low, rises and cools, bringing clouds. In a high pressure system, also called a high, the air slowly sinks, warming up and drying out.

Making a barometer
Barometers measure air pressure. Forecasters use a mercury barometer or an aneroid (airless) one. You can make your own barometer.

You will need
a glass jar
a balloon
a strong elastic band
a straw
tape or glue
thin card
plasticine
a felt-tip pen

1. Cut off the narrow top of a balloon. Stretch the large round part tightly over the top of a wide-mouthed glass jar. Use a strong elastic band to keep it in place.

2. With tape or glue, fix one end of the straw to the centre of the stretched balloon.

3. Stick a piece of card to the side of the jar with plasticine. Make sure the card is big enough to mark the position of the straw on it. Mark a scale in centimetres or inches above and below the position of the straw. Do not set your barometer in the sun or near a radiator.

high pressure

low pressure

As the air pressure changes, the balloon will puff up or go limp. This will move the straw down or up. If the air pressure is high, the air outside the jar will become heavier than the air inside. This will cause the balloon to be pushed into the jar. The straw will rise. This usually means fair weather. If the pressure is lower, the balloon will puff up. The straw will go down. That means rain may be on the way.

As changes occur in the weather, mark the card according to where the straw points.

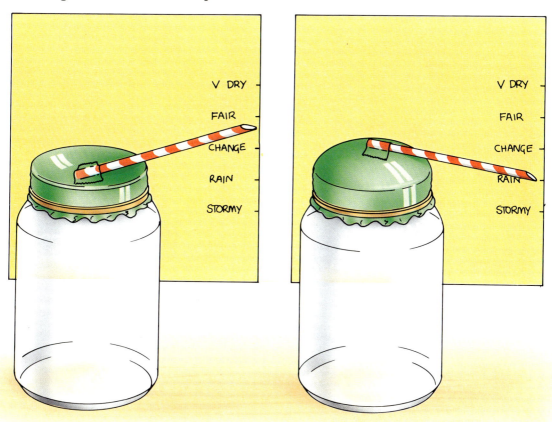

Measuring Temperature

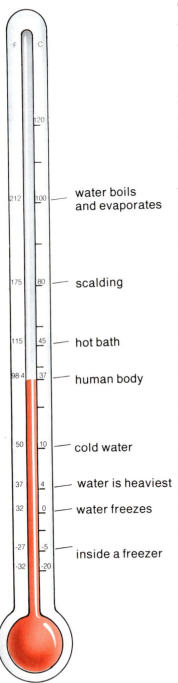

Thermometers are used to measure the air temperature, which is a very important part of the weather.

Most thermometers consist of a fine glass tube filled with mercury. Mercury is a liquid metal that expands when it is heated. As the mercury expands and contracts, it moves up and down the tube. The tube is marked with a scale.

There are two scales for measuring temperature – the Fahrenheit scale and the Celsius, or centigrade, scale. In the Fahrenheit scale, water freezes at 32 degrees. In the Celsius scale, it freezes at 0 degrees.

Weather forecasters use maximum-and-minimum thermometers which record the highest and lowest temperature over a given period. They keep these thermometers in boxes with slatted sides called Stevenson's screens. These compartments shade the instruments so that the temperature of the air can be accurately recorded.

As skiers know, the sun can be burning hot even on a freezing cold day. And sunbathers know how chilling a wind can be, even on the hottest day.

If you want to measure the temperature, you can use an ordinary thermometer. Hang it up where it is out of the sun and out of the wind. Record the temperature when you get up in the morning, at mid-day and in the evening. Notice whether it is rainy, cloudy or fair. Is there a pattern?

Nature's Forecasters

Using man-made equipment is not the only way to predict the weather. Nature provides some very good forecasters.

A clump of seaweed becomes dry and crisp on a fair day. Then, before a rainstorm, the seaweed will become damp and clammy again. Pine cones open and close according to the weather. If a cone closes, wet weather is probably on the way. If a cone dropped its seeds in rainy weather, they would be too heavy with dampness to blow away to find a new place to grow. When the air dries, the pine cone opens up. It tries to spread its seeds to the farthest reaches possible.

Other plants also wait for dry weather before they let go of their seeds. Look for a fern that has spore capsules, which look like little dark dots, on the underside of its fronds.

1. Take a capsule from the back of the fern leaf and place it on a white piece of paper.

2. Use the magnifying glass to study the capsule. Notice that it is divided into different tiny sections.

3. Shine the torch on the capsule until it begins to heat up. Do the tiny sections open to release their spores?

4. Fill the dropper with water. Drip a little on to the open capsule. Did the sections snap shut again? Why?

You will need
a fern with spore capsules
white paper
a magnifying glass
a torch
a dropper

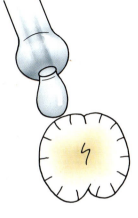

Weather Chart

Now that you know how to make your own weather instruments, you can set up a weather station of your own and use it to make a permanent record of the weather.

Meteorologists show cloud cover in eighths of the sky like this:

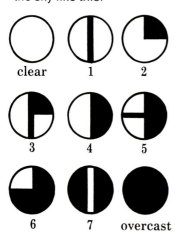

Use your equipment to check temperature, wind direction and strength, and the amount of rain. Keep a daily weather log, using your own readings and information from the television or newspaper. Try to mark your chart at the same time each day. You may also want to keep a weekly or monthly weather chart. You can record the rainfall, the average temperature and the number of clear or cloudy days.

Keep your log in an exercise book or file. You can use graphs or pie charts to record your weather records. You can take photographs of cloud types and stick those in, too. You can add comments about special weather conditions or happenings, like thunderstorms or hurricanes.

One standard way of measuring the wind is with the Beaufort wind scale:		
Beaufort Scale	**Observable Effects**	**Speed (km/h)**
0 Calm		
1 Light air	Drift of smoke	1-5
2 Slight breeze	Leaves rustle, flags stir, wind felt on face	6-11
3 Gentle breeze	Leaves and twigs in constant motion	12-19
4 Moderate breeze	Dust and small branches move, flags flap	20-29
5 Fresh breeze	Small trees sway, flags ripple	30-36
6 Strong breeze	Large branches move, flags flap	37-49
7 Near gale	Whole trees sway, flags extended	50-60
8 Gale	Twigs break off, walking is difficult	61-73
9 Severe gale	Damage to houses, slates dislodged, fences blown over	74-86
10 Storm	Trees uprooted, major damage to houses	87-100
11 Violent storm	Widespread damage	101-120
12 Hurricane	Extensive damage	121-

June 3-9	MON	TUES	WED	THURS	FRI	SAT	SUN
Temperature in °C at 12 noon	22	23	21	19	25	26	27
Cloudy or Sunny	◕	○	◕	◐	◕	○	○
Pressure	change	high	change	low	change	high	high
Rain (or Snow)	—	—	—	7mm	—	—	—
Wind	1	0	2	2	2	0	1
Wind direction	W	—	W	SW	SW	—	SW
Remarks	pressure rising	misty morning, lovely sunny day	rather humid afternoon	rained heavily all day	hot today	even hotter	very humid

JUNE	WEEK 1	WEEK 2	WEEK 3	WEEK 4
Average mid-day temperature in °C	23			
Average cloud cover	◕			
Pressure	change			
Wind	mostly slight			
Direction	mostly SW			
Average Rainfall	1mm			
Remarks	Dry and hot apart from Thursday			

Harnessing the Weather

Scientists are looking at ways to use the weather, to help us and the Earth's environment at the same time? We need electricity and fuel. If we let nature help us, we can produce energy that is clean and safe. Windmills can produce electricity. Solar panels capture the sun's warmth to heat homes and water. We can use water power or hydro-electricity by harnessing rivers, tides and the ocean's waves.

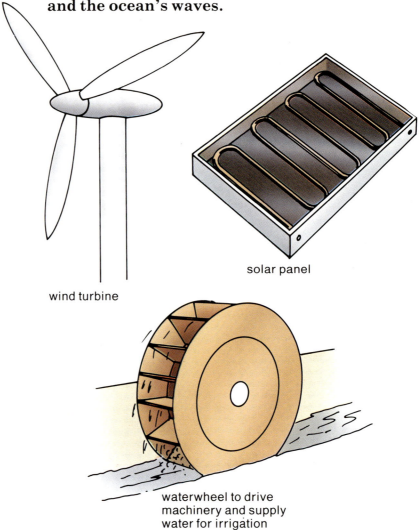

wind turbine

solar panel

waterwheel to drive machinery and supply water for irrigation

Can you think of ways that help save energy? Can you walk or ride your bike rather than being driven? Does your home have insulation?

Government policies can make a big difference in the campaign to help develop alternative sources of energy using weather. But governments cannot do it alone. All of us need to do everything we can to save energy. Each of us has a responsibility to protect our environment. In protecting the Earth and its weather, we also protect ourselves.

Hydro-electric power generated by the huge turbines in a dam like this is a cheap, clean form of energy. But some dams have caused unforseen environmental problems.

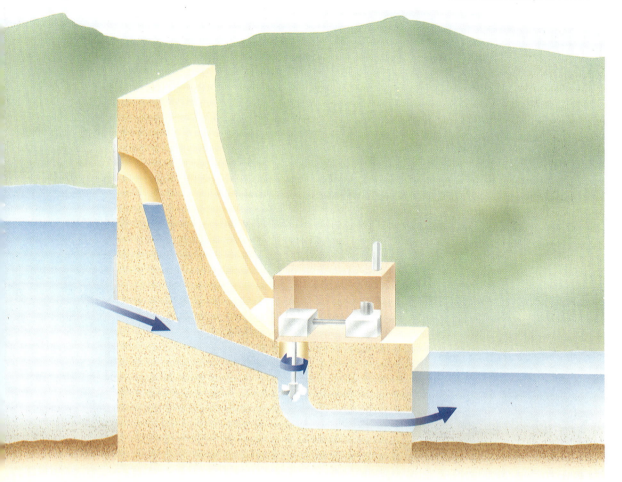

Safety Notes

The projects and experiments in this book are designed to show how certain principles of science work. Most of them are simple to do. Some of them should not be done without permission from an adult. These experiments are marked with this symbol:

It is a good idea to ask permission in any case. You should also make sure that an adult is available to answer any questions that you have.

Some projects are marked with the symbol: (A)

DO NOT TRY TO DO THESE UNLESS YOU HAVE AN ADULT AVAILABLE TO HELP YOU.

Good scientists are very careful. They always protect themselves and other people. They listen to good advice. If you follow the rules given here, you should always stay safe.

Starting work
Before you begin, read the instructions. This will help you understand what must be done. Read the list of materials that you need. Collect everything on the list and put it in one place before you start. Some experiments need some preparation, such as cutting things out or measuring and weighing. Do this first. Remember to get permission if you need it.

Heat, fire and electricity
Some of the projects may involve the use of heat or a flame. Anything that is hot can burn you. Never play with fire, heat or electricity.
  Remember that fire is always dangerous. Always ask an adult to help with experiments in which you need to use a cooker or the flame from a candle. Use only safety matches. Place all your materials so that you do not need to reach across a flame. Do not wear loose clothing that could accidentally get caught in the flame. Keep a pail or jug of water close by just in case.
  If you are using electricity, always ask an adult to keep an eye on you. Remember that mains electricity can kill.

Sharp edges
Some of the projects may involve the use of scissors or knives. Objects with sharp edges are dangerous. Always ask an adult to help with these experiments. Get them to cut out things that you need for a project. Be very careful when opening tins or using mirrors.

Remember that glass breaks easily and broken glass has sharp edges. Most of the projects can be done using plastic jars and glasses. If you do break a glass, get someone to help clear it up immediately.

Chemicals
Some of the projects may involve the use of chemicals. All the chemicals used in this book are harmless household substances, but all chemicals should be treated with respect. Make sure that all containers of chemicals are labelled clearly. Keep them out of the reach of small children and inquisitive animals. Never mix chemical substances unless you are sure that you know what will happen. Some harmless chemicals can become dangerous when they are mixed together. Make sure that you dispose of your chemicals when you have finished the experiment. Wrap dry substances in old newspaper and throw them away. Pour liquids down the sink or an outside drain and flush them away thoroughly with plenty of clean water.

Tools and equipment
Tools such as hammers and nails or drills can cause injury. Always ask an adult for help if you need to use tools in an experiment. They can help you nail or glue things together or drill holes or cut things out.

General rules for safe science
* If in doubt, ask for help from an adult.
* Always wash your hands before you start and when you finish.
* Cover your work surface with old newspapers to protect it.
* Never do any experiment without careful planning. Never try an experiment just to see what will happen.
* You can collect useful objects such as empty containers, card or paper, pencils, etc, to help you in your experiments. Always make sure they are clean. Store them neatly in a convenient place.
* It is a good idea to keep a notebook of your experiments. Take notes after you have done an experiment. Your notes will be useful in the future. If you find that an experiment does not work, your notes will help you understand why. Then you can try the experiment again.
* Always clear everything up after you have finished your experiment. Put away any materials that are left and put any equipment that you have used back where it belongs. Throw away any rubbish.
* Keep dangerous objects and substances out of the reach of smaller children and animals.

Words to Remember

air pressure the weight of air molecules pushing against each other and against the Earth

alternative energy sources of energy, such as wind, water and sun, which do not pollute the Earth's atmosphere

anemometer an instrument for measuring the force and speed of the wind

atmosphere the air surrounding the Earth

average the mean or median value, such as the average temperature of a given region, calculated by adding together two or more quantities and dividing the total by the number of quantities

barometer instrument for measuring air pressure, used in forecasting the weather

cirrus high, thin cloud, usually in white fleecy patches

climate the average weather conditions of a particular region; or a region with specific weather conditions, such as a tropical climate

clouds a visible body of fine drops of water or ice particles in the air

condensation the process in which a gas changes into a liquid

cumulus large white, fluffy cloud

data facts and information organised in a way that makes them easy to analyze

environment conditions that surround us and influence our lives

evaporation the process in which a liquid changes into a vapour, or gas

fog cloudy mass of condensed water vapour lying very close to the ground

forecaster a person who predicts the weather

gas form of matter that is neither liquid nor solid; vapour

gravity the force which pulls all objects towards the Earth

hail round lumps of ice that sometimes fall from clouds during storms. Hailstones can cause serious destruction to crops and property.

hemisphere half of a round object; the Earth is divided into the northern and southern hemispheres, and also into eastern and western hemispheres

high pressure large amount of atmospheric pressure pushing on the Earth's surface; also name for particular type of weather system; see also Low Pressure

humidity the amount of moisture in the atmosphere; dampness

hurricane severe tropical storm with very strong winds

hydro-electricity electricity produced by the power of running water

isobar line of a weather map connecting points of equal air pressure

lightning a powerful flash of light that accompanies a natural electrical discharge in the atmosphere

liquid fluid, flowing substance, not fixed or solid

low pressure small amount of atmospheric pressure pushing on Earth's surface; also name for particular type of weather system; see also High Pressure

meteorologist a scientist specialising in weather and weather conditions

moisture dampness, especially that caused by water vapour in the air

molecule the simplest structural unit or "building block" of matter

pollution an unclean substance which contaminates other substances; for example, chemicals in air or water

rain round drops of water that fall from clouds

rainbow an arc of colours appearing as a result of the refraction, or bending, of sunlight in raindrops or mist

sleet frozen drops of rain that fall from clouds in cold weather

smog air pollution. The word is formed by combining "smoke" and "fog".

snow frozen crystals of water vapour that fall from clouds when the temperature in the cloud is below freezing

stratus low cloud formation spreading out in a long layer

temperature relative hotness or coldness measured on a standard scale

thermometer instrument for measuring temperature

thunder the explosive or rumbling sound following a discharge of lightning

tornado a violently destructive whirlwind

water cycle water's never-ending journey as it rises from Earth and then falls back again

water vapour water in the atmosphere which is invisible

weather the state of the atmosphere at a given time and place. It includes temperature, pressure, humidity, wind and cloudiness

weather front a particular state of the atmosphere, such as a cold front or warm front

weather vane an instrument that turns freely to indicate the direction in which the wind is blowing

whirlwind a small, often violently whirling, column of air

wind moving air

Books to Read

Air in Action by Robin Kerrod   Cherrytree Press   1988
Weather by Michael Cooper   Granada   1983
Weather by Daniel Rogers   Cherrytree Press   1989
Weather by Martyn Bramwell   Franklin Watts   1987
Weather by Ian A Morrison   Ladybird Books   1985
Weather by Gotz Weihmann, translated by Patricia Green   Hart-Davis   1981
Just Look at Weather by John & Mary Gribbin   Macdonald Educational   1985
A Guide to the Weather by Francis Wilson   Usborne Books   1979
Water by Alfred Leutscher   Methuen/Walker Books   1983
Storm by Brian Knapp   Macmillan   1989
Drought by Brian Knapp   Macmillan   1989
Focus on Air by Angela & Derek Lucas   Methuen Children's Books   1977
It's Snowing! by Laurie Bolwell   Wayland Books   1985
The Seasons series by Ralph Whitlock   Wayland Books   1986
Meteorology by Heinz Wachter   Collins Publishers/Franklin Watts   1973
Superbook of Our Planet   Kingfisher Books   1986
The Greenhouse Effect by Philip Neal   Dryad Press   1987
Energy from Sun, Wind & Tide by Jacqueline Dineen   Young Library   1985
The Science Book by Sara Stein   Heinemann   1979
The All Year Round series by Kathleen Edwards   Macdonald and Company   1987
Why Things Are general editor: Lesley Firth   Kingfisher Books   1989
Beginning to Learn about Science by Richard L Allington PhD and Kathleen Krull   Blackwell Raintree Ltd   1983
Simple Science Experiments by Eiji and Masako Orii   Gareth Stevens Children's Books   1989
Longman Illustrated Science Dictionary   1981
Science for Life by Bishop, Maddocks and Scott   Collins Educational   1984
Life on Earth by Linda Gamlin   Gloucester Press   1988

Index

air 13, 14, 16, 17, 18, 20, 23, 24, 25, 32, 35, 36, 37
air pressure 7, 13, 14, 15, 24, 27, 34, 35
alternative energy 40-41
anemometer 29
animals 8
atmosphere 13, 24, 32
atmospheric pressure 13, 24

barometer 34-35

Celsius 36
centigrade 36
chart, weather 38-39
cirrus clouds 21, 22
climate 7
clouds 7, 19, 20, 21-23, 24, 27, 38
   cirrus 21, 22 cumulus 21, 22
   stratus 21, 22
cold 16, 17, 18, 19, 21
condensation 20, 21
crystals, ice 22, 32
cumulus clouds 21, 22

Earth 10, 11, 13, 20, 32
electricity 40, static 32
energy 40-41
environment 40-41
evaporation 18, 20, 22

Fahrenheit 36
fern 37
fog 23
forecasting 27, 34, 35, 36, 37
freezing 22, 36
friction 32

gases 13, 18, 22
hail 22
hailstones 22
heat 8, 9, 16, 17, 18, 20, 21, 24, 32, 36
humidity 18, 24, 38
hurricane 24
hydro-electricity 40

ice 18, 22, 32

life 8, 9
light 8
lightning 32, 33

measuring weather 27
mercury 36
meteorologist 27
moisture 7, 18, 21
molecule 13, 16, 20, 21

pine cone 37
plants 8-9
pollen 38
pollution 32

rain 20, 22, 27, 30, 31, 35, 37, 38
rain gauge 30

seasons 12
seaweed 37
shadow 10-11
sleet 22
smog 23
snow 20, 22
snowflakes 22

solar energy 40
spores 37
static electricity 32
Stevenson's screen 36
stratus clouds 21, 22
sun 7, 8, 10, 11, 18, 20, 24
sundial 10-11
sunlight 8-9, 27, 38

temperature 7, 21, 22, 27, 32, 36, 38
thermometer 36 Celsius scale 36 Fahrenheit scale 36
thunder 32
thundercloud 22, 32
thunderstorm 32
time 10-11
tornado 24
turbines 40

water 9, 18, 19, 20, 21, 23, 32
water cycle 20
water droplets 22, 32
water power 40
water vapour 18, 20, 21, 23, 24
water wheel 40
weather chart 38-39
weather station 38
weather systems 32
wind 7, 24, 25, 26, 27, 29, 38
windmill 26, 40
wind vane 28